Friend

Pauletta Hansel

DOS MADRES

2020

DOS MADRES PRESS INC.
P.O. Box 294, Loveland, Ohio 45140
www.dosmadres.com   editor@dosmadres.com

Dos Madres is dedicated to the belief that the small press is essential to the vitality of contemporary literature as a carrier of the new voice, as well as the older, sometimes forgotten voices of the past. And in an ever more virtual world, to the creation of fine books pleasing to the eye and hand.

Dos Madres is named in honor of Vera Murphy and Libbie Hughes, the "Dos Madres" whose contributions have made this press possible.

Dos Madres Press, Inc. is an Ohio Not For Profit Corporation and a 501 (c) (3) qualified public charity. Contributions are tax deductible.

Executive Editor: Robert J. Murphy

Illustration & Book Design: Elizabeth H. Murphy
www.illusionstudios.net

Typeset in Adobe Garamond Pro. Dali & Prestige Elite
ISBN 978-1-953252-16-6
Library of Congress Control Number: 2020949783

First Edition
Copyright 2020 Pauletta Hansel
All rights reserved. No part of this book may be reproduced or transmitted in any form or by any means graphic, electronic or mechanical, including photocopying, recording, taping or by any information storage or retrieval system, without the permission in writing from the publisher.
Published by Dos Madres Press, Inc.

For Chuck, Roberta and Erica,
    the friends whose poems
 called these poems into being:

"Because you are the only person I can talk with about the shade of a cloud, about the song of a thought — and about how, when I went out to work today and looked a tall sunflower in the face, it smiled at me with all of its seeds."

(Vladimir Nabokov)

To write just because the poet wants to write is natural,
but to learn to see is a blessing.
—Linda Gregg

"YOU MUST STOP MOVING….Forsake the Open Road…
You Do not "Advance," You only Trample…"
—The Angel, *Angels in America* (Tony Kushner)

"What is a week end?"
—The Dowager Countess, *Downton Abby*

Table of Contents

Foreword..........................ix

March 16, 2020.....................1
March 17, 2020.....................2
March 18, 2020.....................3
March 20, 2020.....................4
March 22, 2020.....................5
March 23, 2020.....................7
March 24, 2020.....................8
March 27, 2020.....................9
April 2, 2020.....................10
April 5, 2020.....................11
April 7, 2020.....................16
April 8, 2020.....................17
April 10, 2020....................18
April 13, 2020....................19
April 15, 2020....................20
April 20, 2020....................21
April 25, 2020....................22
May 1, 2020.......................25
June 2, 2020......................28
June 17, 2020.....................29

Notes.............................30
Acknowledgements..................31
About the Author..................33

Foreword

On March, 4, 2020, when my *From Draft to Craft* Poetry Class started back for the year, I announced the theme for the Spring Session was Epistolary Poetry, inviting each member to pair up with another for an exchange of letter poems. I offered as inspiration the Nabokov quote from *Letters to Vera* that is on the dedication page of this book. Little did we know that this sharing would become our primary mode of communication with each other; within a few days of our second gathering, shelter-in-place orders were declared in our community. The Epistolary Poetry Project became more than just a generative poetry activity, though it certainly was that. It also was a source of creative and emotional strength and support as we navigated the new world in which we found ourselves in this time of the global pandemic.

The poems in this book are my part of the conversation with three of the poets, Chuck Stringer, Roberta Schultz and Erica Manto Paulson. I invite you to read samples of their poems, and those of other Cincinnati area poets on my website at:

https://paulettahansel.wordpress.com/home/postcards-from-the-pandemic-cincinnati-poetry-month-2020/.

I will note that the final two poems in *Friend* were written more than a month after the class ended, when I found that direct address to beloved friends was how I could best speak my difficult truths.

These poems would not exist without the class and these three poets in particular, and this book would not exist without Rebecca Gayle Howell, who encouraged the collection and provided essential editorial advice. My deep gratitude to these poets, and to Robert and Elizabeth Murphy of Dos Madres Press.

Friend, I hope you will find the poems within engaging both as poetry, and as a record of this historic time.

Friend

```
March 16, 2020
```

Friend, do you believe kindness
             is enough? I want to hold your answer
close to me, feel your warmth.
             I am never warm enough
these days. I want to love the gray.
             I want to say gray
is my blank page, the only way to begin.
             Let me begin again, friend.
Yesterday I drove through sky, the ground
             a mirror to the clouds. Here and there
the purple fallow fields—
             henbit, deadnettle up
before the planting. It grows; it's plowed away.
             I want, I want is all I know to say.
All around us purple waves of wanting—
             the grocery shelves, picked clean.
A flock of turkey buzzards rises up, sated.
             Do you believe we'll learn
to take enough?

March 17, 2020

Have you noticed how the skin we've worn
            six decades now is not so quick to heal?
The bruise, faint shadow just above my wrist bone,
            may be yesterday's sharp falter,
or last week's.
            Friend, I can hardly remember last week.
We sat, legs dangling from the edge.
            I dreamed last night a flock of flamingos overhead.
You would think this a good omen,
            but they let loose a poison cloud of excrement,
shadowing my view.
            This morning, I walk out to what was garden
looking for green's thrust.
            As in any March there is the ordinary
miracle of rhizome and bulb.
            The magnolia has just begun its bloom,
a seam of carnival pink against brown wool,
            and your poem pings my Inbox.
You write you welcome my reply
            come Monday next.
I trust your welcome will extend itself to now,
            when I can still remember what is here today.

March 18, 2020

I am spending a lot of time in cemeteries,
            these days. No risk hurting anybody,
the earth's greening plods along as always
            as I walk the blacktop road;
the dogwood's buttoned tight
            down the branches.
Everybody tucked in place. Last night I dreamed
            it was my mother calling
on the red phone beside my bed. Until I'd laid down
            the receiver with its satisfying clunk,
I had forgotten
            she was dead. Awake, I never forget.
All over the internet daughters, sisters, wives
            are locked outside the nursing home door.
The newspapers say those who die
            are mostly dying alone.
In the end, the only speech my mother knew:
            touch.
Friend, if I could find her on the other side
            of the corded line, I'd say, I miss you.
I don't wish you were here.

March 20, 2020

Friend, this morning's walk: a search for wildness.
                      Last year's nest of hornets
lists precarious from a neighbor's Bradford Pear.
                      Scrub brush greens on a narrow ridge of clay
the bulldozer unearthed.
                      I stop and think about that word,
Unearth.
                      Is that not the art we've tried to master?
Last night, tornado sirens;
                      today sidewalks slicked with mud
that slipped the walls between hillside and street.
                      The life I lived just days ago—
the clink of other people's cutlery—
                      seems as strange to me now
as pictures of the wildlife market,
                      the stacked cages,
claw and beak and blood-matted fur.

March 22, 2020

Friend, did you see the sun,
          a gift, remembered brightness
at the end of the day.
          I stood at the fence talking
to a tree, my husband reported
          from his window;
from my view, to a neighbor
          about raised garden beds and squirrels
who keep no distance
          from our tulips and tomatoes.
How sweet to complain
          of ordinary losses,
the stubbornness of squirrels,
          a lilac tree that has again this year
refused us blossoms.

March 23, 2020

Yesterday's kindness—a gray fish
    in a puddle of river
along the concrete path.
    My husband
scooped her in a torn Styrofoam cup,
    returned her to the water,
receded now into its banks.
    Carp, he said.
If this were a tale, she would be
    a silver trout with wishes.
Not even a thank you, my husband said.
    Pestilence. Flood. Next
comes locusts
    or is it the volcano in Yellowstone
about to spew ash on our sorry heads?
    Downstream
we read scrawled on the floodwall:
    *We are a balloon
in a world full of pins.*
    I say we are the pins,
this earth, soft beneath us.

March 24, 2020

Have I ever told you my mother
             cancelled her newspaper subscription
when for the second time that ice-swathed winter
             delivery was delayed? I think about this
while my husband labors to repair
             on my computer those things invisible
I never knew I needed till they failed me.
             And how I wake at night,
the chatter at the open window
             of my brain—*she did, he said, they never will*—
My father held his grudges close,
             poor substitute for love
his alcoholic father never turned his way.
             When hurt is all that's handed down
you learn to claim it.
             And so I see you, friend,
inside the poem you sent me,
             kneeling in your spring damp garden,
gloves on your quick hands
             as you pull leaves from last year's
Lenten roses, looking for
             the middle way my family never found,
to let it live, what's tender green inside;
             to let them go, those jagged bits
of what's already gone.

March 27, 2020

Counting. That's how to get through.
              But you have to know what to count.
The number of days
              since you entered a door not your own. (Six.)
The steps you take, the miles. (Eight).
              The hands that have touched you. (Two.)
Some people count toilet paper rolls in the bathroom closet.
              I count poems, trees newly blossomed
on my twice-daily walks. (See miles, above).
              The feet I stand from my neighbor. (Ten.)
The news counts the sick and the dead.
              I try not to count the degrees of separation
between us, friend.
              The hellebore blooms in my front garden.
The daffodils in back. (Thirty.)
              The times I raise my hand in greeting.
The hours of sun, but not the days of rain.

April 2, 2020

Dear friend,
           On March 26, you wrote,
With every curse a little blessing.
               I've said myself there is no shadow
without light. But does it work the other way?
           On yesterday's walk—from the neighbor's tall grasses,
a sudden flash of mottled brown. Midstride,
        I grab my husband's arm as a hawk flies
past our faces to another neighbor's pine.
        A blessing, surely.
This time together in the greening spring,
           rounding the corner on our urban sidewalk
to see what we otherwise would not.
          Not so much a blessing for the mouse.

April 5, 2020

At first I think they are everywhere,
    the Bradford Pears, their gaudy, gauzy
tutu white against a mostly leafless landscape,
    one more dubious pleasure of this spring,
like our weekend trips to bike paths for walks we could,
    yes, take as our own urban sidewalks,
and do, and do, and do—
    but then I notice,
or maybe my husband says it first,
    that the pears cluster where the people are;
where the endless tracts
    of end-of-millennium look-alike houses end,
the pears end too.

⸻

Here's a little known fact, friend.
    The first seeds for what became,
in our hands, the Bradford Pear,
    made their way down the Yangtze
from Yichang to what is now Wuhan
    in 1918
in the bags of a plant explorer
    hired by the US Department of Agriculture.
The seeds were shipped to Washington
    after the explorer's body was fished from the river.
Suicide, they think.
    "Few people ever realized
the tremendous battle that was raging in his soul,"
    wrote the plant scientist who'd sent him.
Not about the seeds, surely, but interesting nonetheless.

———·····———

We all want to blame somebody, and that's a fact.
    Millennials are blaming the boomers
and my friend in the UK posts,
    "People of America. I swear to god. Stay at home,"
and our sorry excuse for a President
    calls it the China Virus.
I want to blame somebody, too, so I yell at my husband
    for not fixing the damn windshield wipers
back in January
    when we still had someplace to go in the rain,
or anytime we damn well wanted,
    damn it.

———·····———

"Without thinking much about it,
    we have globalized our environment
in much the same way
    we have globalized our economy."
Peter Del Tredici,
    Harvard senior research scientist, retired

———·····———

"The coronavirus can live for three days on plastic and steel
  and travel through the air suspended
for about a half-hour."
  The New York Times

———·····———

"Seed longevity likely contributes
                    to the invasive tendencies of
[the Bradford] pear,
                  enabling it to persist
despite efforts at surface-level removal."
                  Scientists Theresa Culley and Tziporah Serotain

———— ····· ————

It's not the seeds that are to blame.
                It's 100 years later in the Hubei Provence
and the pear trees there
                have stayed in their place.
We took and selected, propagated and fused,
                and planted them wherever we wanted
something pretty that we didn't have to wait for,
                that would look just like the ones our neighbors had
but maybe bigger.
                It's hard to say which we I am talking about.
Scientists agree that the SARS-CoV-2,
        AKA COVID-19,
AKA novel coronavirus,
        AKA the virus,
was the result of natural selection.
                So at least we didn't make the thing on purpose,
like we did the Bradford Pear,
                the perfect tree.
But there's more than one way
                to engineer a pandemic.
I reckon the pangolins
                would rather have stayed deep inside their forests
if there were still forests
                where they used to stay.

Friend, it's hard to stay home.
                But mostly we do.
Twice daily walks around the neighborhood,
                and on what we still call weekends we sit swaddled
in our car for a while, headed out to the burbs
                to walk along the mostly empty bike paths.
every now and then diving into the brush
                to avoid a gaggle of humans.
We try not to be too smug.
                We try to not say to each other,
"You can't tell me they all live in the same house."
                We try not to feel too guilty
for being out where anyone can see us,
                far from home.

Friend, remember when I said those pears were everywhere?
                Theresa Culley has a theory
and it has to do with robins,
                the Turdus migratorius,
that most American of birds,
                which unlike the European starlings
drop their poop deep inside a forest,
                not just along its edge.
Poop is my word, not Dr. Culley's.

It was May 31, 1918
            when Frank Meyer, plant explorer,
boarded a ship from what is now Wuhan
            to sail downriver to Shanghai,
from where he intended to ship his seeds.
            He had been suffering from a stomach bug,
but seemed much better.
            You are probably already thinking about the virus
we used to call Spanish but remember scientists trace that one
            from an army camp in Kansas
which sent men across the country and on to Europe
            for the sole purpose of killing people,
and that's what they did.

April 7, 2020

It's hard to remember
>anybody dies
of anything else these days,
>but we do.
Cancer and car wrecks,
>strokes and strikes
against the unfevered brow.
>Pneumonia, uncomplicated
by what we mostly call the virus,
>and know which one we mean.
I want to write about something other
>than its daily onslaught.
I want to look forward
>to seeing my husband again
at the end of the day.
>I want to take nothing for granted,
our long walks along the serpentine paths
>of the country's oldest urban golf course—
who knew!—
>which, in normal times,
would be forbidden to my uncleated feet,
>even though I have one of those little skirts
with the shorts sewn in, like the golfing women wear,
>who I never want to be.
Oh, friend, this comfortable life
>of complaints against different and too much same,
our luxury unearned—in the end,
>however it comes,
is not mine to keep.

April 8, 2020

Dear friend, the days pass quickly now.
                Did you think you'd see these words
from me, who just last week—or was it two—
                wrote nostalgia of restaurants and stores?
My husband and I venture
                farther now from home,
shy creatures of the underbrush,
                with face masks and wipes.
I admit to you my inclination
                is to outrun the black dog,
though at 60 I outwalk it.
                Fifty miles last week, my wristwatch says.
I could have walked to Fowlers Fork
                and back again, by now.
I could have stood six feet downstream,
                skipped a stone to you.
The best stone skipper
                chooses her rock with the jeweler's attention.
As in anything, it's practice
                that makes an art of love.

April 10, 2020

Friend, how would you describe the scent
            of a newborn baby?
Salt and blood,
            the woman-slick just begun to dry?
Is it days or weeks until
            she's milk and powder,
soap and wipes to clean away the slick
            that comes from inside her own self now,
coiled worm of bowels?
            Briefly she'll smell of dryer sheets
with names like natural and fresh pine.
            Other times it must be
formula dribbled and dried.
            What words for all that rises
from deep in the small
            caverns of her body?
To me now she is only screen,
            face smooth or scrunched,
no whiff of flesh
            drifting from my phone.
When finally I can breathe her in
            will that make her any more mine?

April 13, 2020

Crabgrass beneath the iris rhizomes
                where my muddy fingers can't tell
one root from another.
                Meanwhile, in the French Quarter
the rats are starving.
                No tourists, no trash.
What can they do but eat their young?
                Everyone wants to survive.
Inside our lungs the virus slips
                itself into the Ace-2 receptors and is reborn.
Scientists call what happens next a cytokine storm.
                Bugler, sound the charge!
An army of cells marches up from the trenches,
                kills what it can't save.
"We have to think about this pandemic
                from the virus's position."
Friend, everyone wants to survive.

April 15, 2020

I don't mean to be ungrateful.
                I was bred for wanting more, the way
a racehorse is bred for the win's scent.
                Those impossible legs like winged twigs
that will snap in a high wind.
                What moves us onward is the same,
sometimes, as what breaks us to the ground.
                Friend, here's a story about my grandfather
that I don't like to tell,
                how he found a WWII deserter's bundle
tucked inside a cave,
                how he kept the money, then turned the guy in
for a $15 reward.
                I'm not saying our people weren't hungry.
We were always hungry.
                I'm not saying who my grandfather was,
is who I am.
                What my mother wanted
was to be far away
                from where she started.
What my father wanted
                was to begin again.
I'm telling you
                the hardest thing
I've ever had to do
                is to stop wanting
what I already have.

April 20, 2020

They say old white men can get away with anything,
              so why am I surprised, middle of the morning,
to see a saggy-jowled man in a red jacket
              pissing behind a shiny black BMW
right there on Reading not too far from Tennessee,
              his hands invisible but fidgeting his zipper
(you can tell by how his elbows
              flap up above the trunk of the car).
Friend, I am walking fast,
              a little faster after that.
I see the things I never would have
              back when I would drive someplace pretty to walk.
It doesn't matter anymore what the sky is doing;
              I am grabbing my corona mask,
getting out of the house.
              Under the train trestle, where Tennessee
turns into Ross,
              still the same purple bra,
but now green weeds push up through its straps,
              and against the concrete wall,
a busted tire splayed open
              looks just like a peacock feather Mardi Gras mask,
iridescent as this puddle of grease and pee.

April 25, 2020

Perhaps all my poems begin with I want,
              and I've learned to make the words
invisible, the way the eye
              behind the camera panning the room
keeps the doorway to her back.
              We are all in the room, friend,
no matter what door we entered.
              We call the room longing;
we are in it together,
              alone.

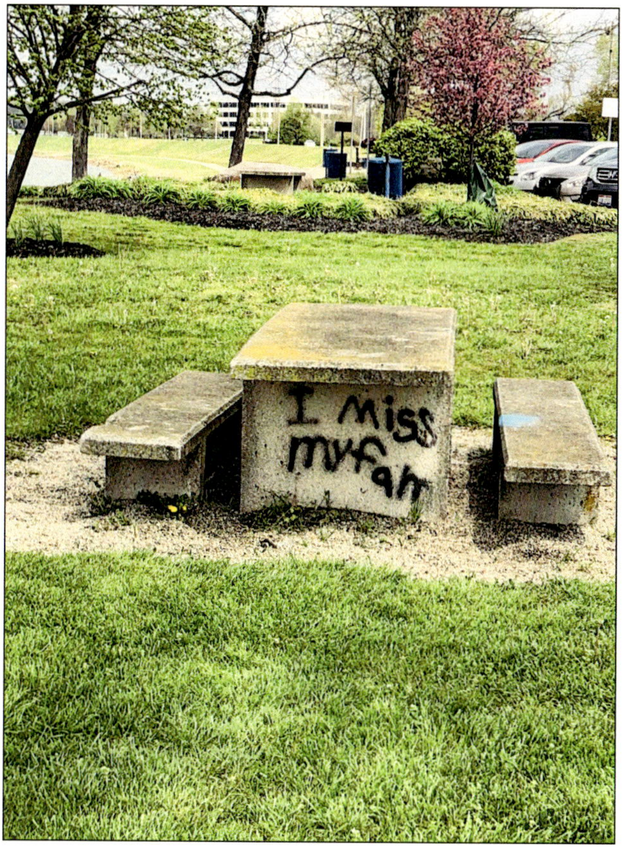
I Miss
my fam

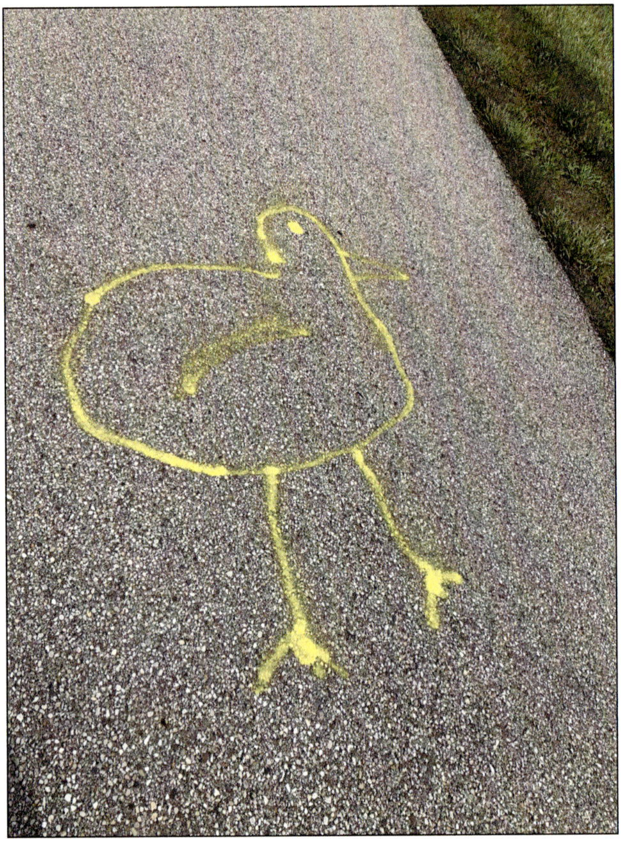

May 1, 2020

My husband, the business analyst,
          has such good ideas for what I should do
these days. Yesterday, it was an online limerick workshop.
          Today, as we walk the bike trail along the river,
even the geese social distancing,
          waddling away in their family units,
he says I should write a book, *The Birds of the Great Miami.*
          All I know of birds would fit in a limerick.
He is trying to make me laugh,
          so I do, but I keep my thoughts on the birds.
The red-winged blackbird we hear before we see,
          having learned his *chit, chit, chit la ree*
on a muddy March walk
          in a fen—a word we had to look up
on the internet which bid us look down
          to the cattails for a startle of red.
Map-challenged seagulls dive the puny waves;
          the turkey vultures circle the path,
waiting for our stumble.
          I am a little weary, I admit;
five miles forward, five miles back
          to where I started from.
Friend, what else is there to do
          but learn to use the word undulating in a sentence;
no other way to name the wind's pull and release
          of tall grasses between us and the river,
while the blotches of clouds overhead
          are still as if the vultures revolve in a virtual sky
behind a Zoom meeting
          instead of a life.
On the cracked asphalt trail
          someone has chalked a tweety bird,

The token bird of the Great Miami,
              I joke,
but the red-winged black bird is the totem I claim
                for us. Farther along,
the artist wrote, in the same yellow chalk,
                    fainter now, words fading into the path:
"We will be OK."

WE WILL BE OK

June 2, 2020

Friend, you still walk your stretch of creek,
              though what was flood in spring
is a languid, muddy trickle
              in this early summer drought.
And I still trudge gray city sidewalks
              looking for the words.
You heave flat rocks
              up to the bank of Fowlers Fork;
the drystone wall
              you'll build to save its wildness
shapely in your mind.
              I envy you your steadfast labor,
though I admit a thrill to see a wrecking ball's
              square hit against the cornerstone
of what has long been crumbling on our streets.
              A flood is rising from the wounds
we've tried for centuries to ignore.
              Curfews and walls of uniforms
will not contain it. Oh, friend,
              it is so easy to say
that violence is not the answer,
              so much harder to heave all the questions
up from beneath the smooth green lawns
              on which our houses sit.

June 17, 2020

Do you remember
                when the only thing asked of us
was to keep our breath at home?
                Even that was more than we could give.
Even then we were divided—
                those who thought we saved the world
by keeping it outside our doors;
                those who stocked the shelves,
loaded the delivery vans
                that kept the rest of us alive,
then hauled away our stinking excess
                as we slept. Friend, no matter
how little we thought we had,
                it was always too much.

NOTES

March 18, 2020 *The first report of nursing home residents dying alone was in The Washington Post article,* U.S. coronavirus death toll surpasses 100, *March 17, 2020.*

April 5, 2020 *Research about the Bradford Pear mainly came from these sources:* How We Turned the Bradford Pear into a Monster, *The Washington Post, September 14, 2018 and* The Detested Bradford Pear Tree Is Coming to a Forest Near You, *citylab.com, July 2, 2019.*

April 13, 2020 *Quote from virologist Mike Skinner of Imperial College London in The Guardian, April 12, 2020.*

May 1, 2020 *Many of us are hoping to go back, eventually, to some kind of normal, but for artists…there is nothing there… to "go back" to. You are the job.*—The Coronavirus Means Curtains for Artists, William Deresiewicz, *The Nation*

ACKNOWLEDGEMENTS

Versions of the following poems have appeared or are forthcoming in:

Sleet Magazine (**March 20, 2020; June 2, 2020; and June 17, 2020**)

The Cincinnati Review MiCRo Series (**March 23, 2020**)

Pudding Magazine #70 (**March 24, 2020**)

One Jacar (**April 5, 2020**)

Lexington Poetry Month Website (**April 10, 2020**)

The New Verse News (**April 13, 2020**)

Psaltery and Lyre (**April 15, 2020**)

Juke Joint Magazine (**April 20, 2020**)

The Oxford American (**May 1, 2020**)

Readings from **March 16, 2020**; **March 18, 2020**; and **April 5, 2020** are included in the virtual exhibit called The Spring Creek Project: *The Nature of Isolation*
https://www.youtube.com/c/SpringCreekProject

Cover art by Loren Crawford
Photographs by Owen P. Cramer

ABOUT THE AUTHOR

PAULETTA HANSEL is a poet, memoirist and teacher who is author of seven poetry collections in addition to *Friend*, including *Coal Town Photograph* and *Palindrome*, winner of the 2017 Weatherford Award for best Appalachian Poetry. Her writing has been widely anthologized and featured in print and online journals including *Oxford American*, *Rattle*, *The Writer's Almanac*, *American Life in Poetry*, *Verse Daily*, *Appalachian Journal*, *Appalachian Review*, *Cincinnati Review*, *Pine Mountain Sand & Gravel*, and *Still: The Journal*, among others. Pauletta was Cincinnati's first Poet Laureate, 2016-2018.

Other books by Pauletta Hansel
published by Dos Madres Press

First Person (2007)
What I Did There (2011)
Tangle (2015)
Palindrome (2017)
Coal Town Photograph (2019)

She is also included in:
Realms of the Mothers:
The First Decade of Dos Madres Press - 2016

For the full Dos Madres Press catalog:
www.dosmadres.com